The ABC of Mazes

The path through a maze is often like the path through life, as the little mazes below show. Sometimes we choose the long way when a more direct path would have been best. Sometimes we have to return to the start to make it to the goal. Sometimes there are many different paths that will get us there. Difficult-looking problems may turn out to be the easiest, while simple-looking ones may be no way out at all! This also teaches us a valuable lesson—namely, you don't always get your money back if things don't work out!

(Solution: page 30)

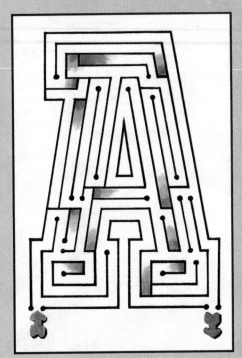
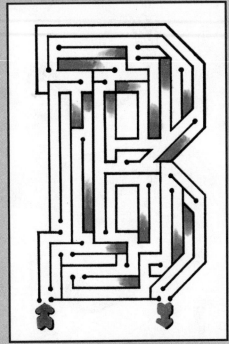
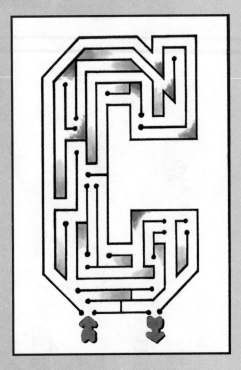

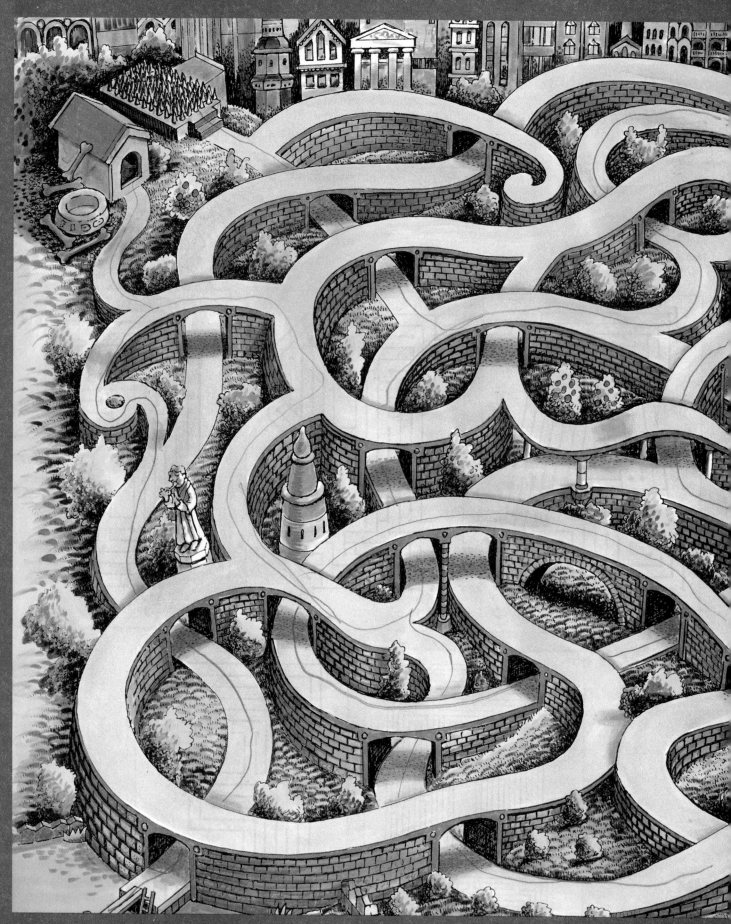

Mazeville

Five characters are on their way home to Mazeville.
Can you guess where they live and help them find their way? (Solution: page 30)

Rolf Heimann's
AMAZING
Head-Spinning
MAZES

Troll

1 easy

2 not so easy

3 a bit hard

4 very hard

First published in the United States in 2000 by Troll Communications L.L.C.

Copyright © 1999 by Rolf Heimann.

Published by arrangement with Roland Harvey Books, Port Melbourne, Victoria, Australia.

ISBN 0-8167-6988-5

Designed by Roland Harvey Studios.

Printed in the United States of America.

10 9 8 7 6 5 4 3 2 1

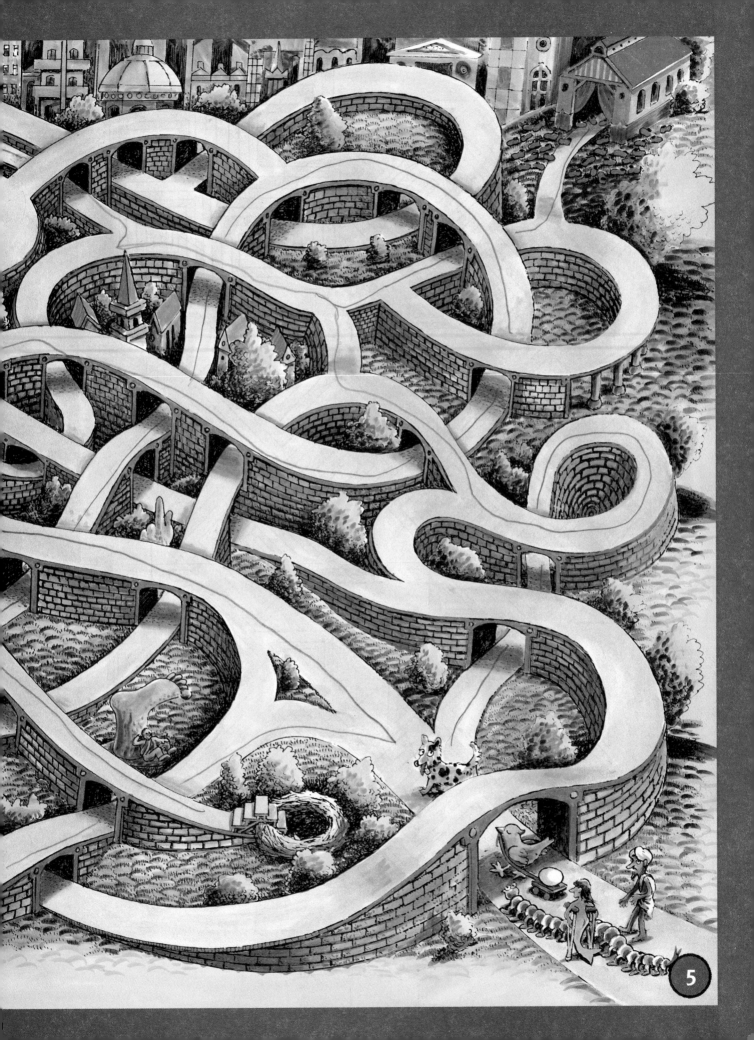

Say Cheese

Five mice are trying to get to the cheese. Will they be able to?

(Solution: page 30)

Pyramid

Imagine the pyramid being unfolded, the base being the black triangle. There are several ways of "unfolding" it, but the arrows must always point to the top and the colors must stay in the same order. Some of the examples are wrong. Which ones?

(Solution: page 30)

Water Castle

Tom, Lila, and Ben arrived in the yellow boat and want to leave in the blue one.
Help them find their way across the island fortress.

b l o o d s h e d

n u t s h e l l

C o m b a t

M o n k e y

E a r n e s t

S k i l l e d

A n t h e m

s t a r c h

H a n d I c a p

C o w a r d i c e

Word Blending

Use two or more words to form a new word
from the list below. Note: Some words, when
combined, share a letter or letters:
EARNEST, ANTHEM, SKILLED, BLOODSHED,
COMBAT, NUTSHELL, MONKEY, COWARDICE,
HATRED, HANDICAP, STARCH, MINESWEEPER.

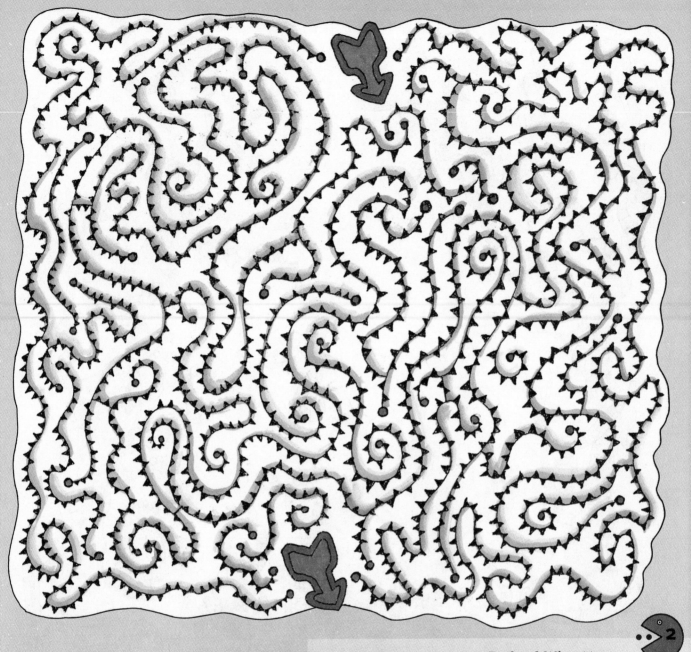

Barbed Wire Maze
Don't get stuck as you go from top to bottom.

Rebus
Here's a hint: If you're a puppy, you might learn something! (Solution: page 30)

Snakesssss!

Snakekeeper Enrico has to take Annabelle the Patagonian Asp for her yearly checkup.
So that he could find her, he brought along Annabelle's picture. But spotting her isn't easy,
is it? Once you find Annabelle, see if you can guess how many snakes there are in this
picture: 27? 41? 53? (Solution: page 30)

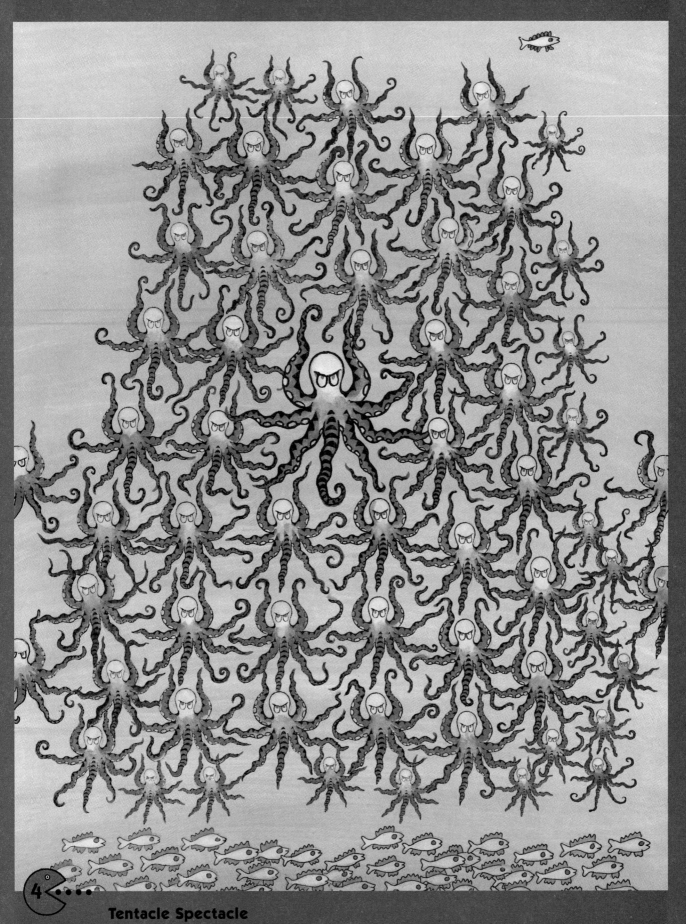

Tentacle Spectacle

Rover the yellow sardine is lost.

Can he find his way back to his school through the maze of tentacles?

(Solution: page 30)

Snap!

Major McKlink has to make an emergency landing on the planet Snappio II, which is inhabited by the multicolored Snapponoids. Luckily they are not as dangerous as they look—the only poisonous ones are the two-colored ones. Those with more than two colors are quite harmless. Is there a two-colored Snapponoid among them?

(Solution: page 30)

Double-Maze

16

There are two ways to get through this maze—either through the hedges in the middle or along the orange path around the outside.

WOOD **IN** ASH
EARLY **B** LATE
GOOD **E** BEST
POLAND **T** FRANCE
EGG **W** FROG
BUD **E** FRUIT
FALL **E** SPRING
SHOULDER **N** HAND
EIGHT **S** TEN
CHEEK CHEEK

(Solution: page 30)

In-Bit-Tweens

There's always something in between. Fill in the right words. For instance, between wood and ash is fire!

Nothing will come between us!

It's the same thing.

And again!

Relativity

Everything is relative! The first answer is given to show you what to do. Don't just fill in the answers, draw the pictures as well. Note: Some of these puzzles have more than one right answer! (Solution: page 30)

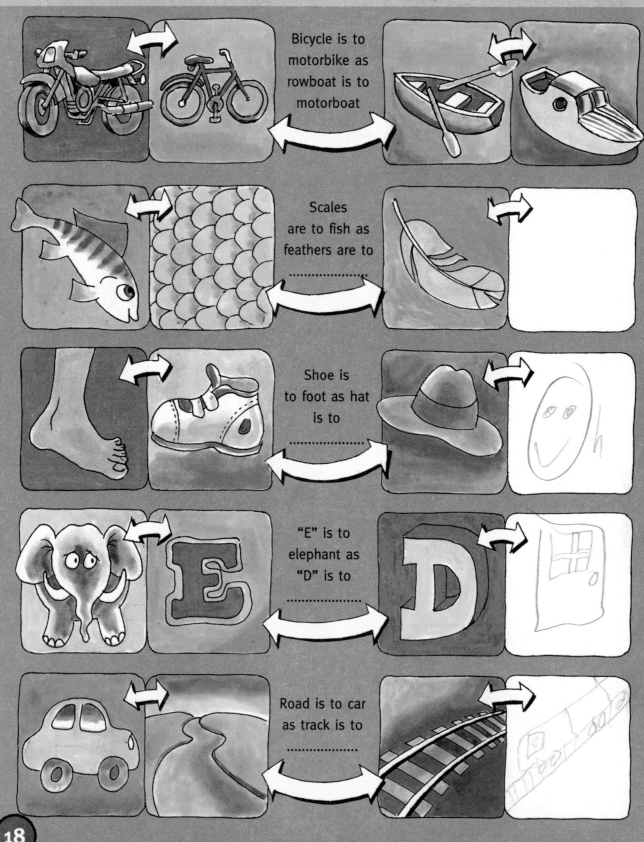

Bicycle is to motorbike as rowboat is to motorboat

Scales are to fish as feathers are to ....

Shoe is to foot as hat is to ....

"E" is to elephant as "D" is to ....

Road is to car as track is to ....

Try making up some on your own! There are a few ideas on page 30.

Dragon Maze

All seven snails will try to make their way through the maze to the leaves on the other side.
Not all of them can! Which ones will make it and which ones will not? (Solution: page 30)

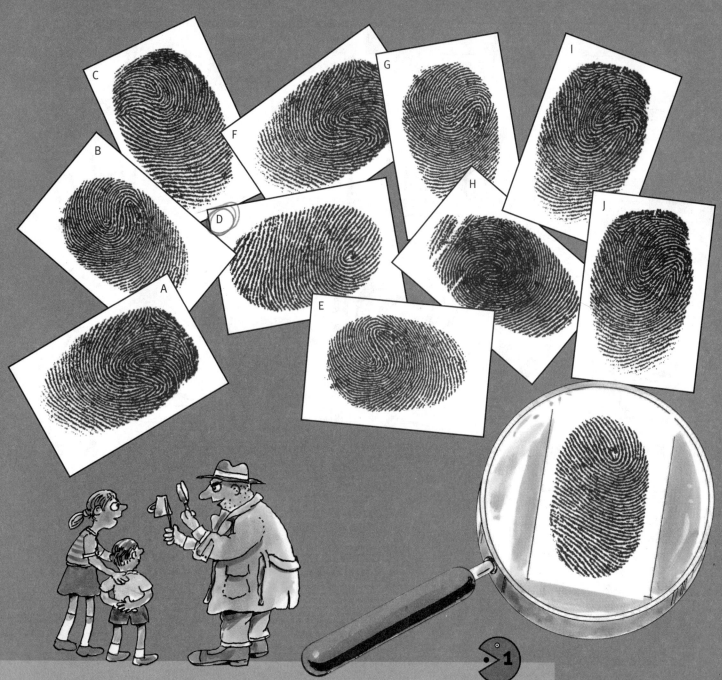

Be a Detective!

Fingerprints are a great means of identification.

One of the ten prints is the same as the one under the magnifying glass.

Which one? Be careful—somebody's life might depend on it!

(Solution: page 31)

Look before you leap

Rhyme and Reason

Rat rhymes with hat! The rat is holding the letter "C," so the "C" goes under the hat. But that's the only clue you'll get for this puzzle. You'll have to find the other rhymes yourself. If you fill in the letters that correspond to each picture, you'll get the name of a U.S. city. We've filled in the first letter to get you started. (Solution: page 31)

Space Captain

Test your memory – or that of your friends! You are the captain of space patrol No. 55, and you are exactly halfway to the galaxy of Nymropia when suddenly another ship appears. A strange green creature from the local Star Watch gets out. According to Intergalactic law, you must answer him truthfully. Before you turn to the next page to read his question, study the picture and this text carefully. If you do, you'll be able to answer.

23

From previous page:
The green creature's question to patrol ship No. 55 is: "What is the name of your captain?"

(Solution: page 31)

24

What's a Gazebo?

The shingles for the gazebo's roof have arrived. But which path should the delivery man take to get there?

What's the opposite of the big-eared Spotted confuscus?

The earless spotless smarticus— which could be me!

•••>3

The Big-Eared Spotted Confuscus

Transfer the lines onto the correct squares below. Use the position of the colored border and the small red squares as your guide.

(Solution: page 31)

25

Upside-Down Pyramid

This upside-down pyramid was built by a tribe of Egyptians who disliked their government so much that they did everything opposite to what was expected. For instance, the tribe did not worship cats but hated them. The sign near the entrance says: "Cats go home."

Can you spot the sign inside the tomb, also in hieroglyphics, that says: "Beware of fools who worship mice"?

26

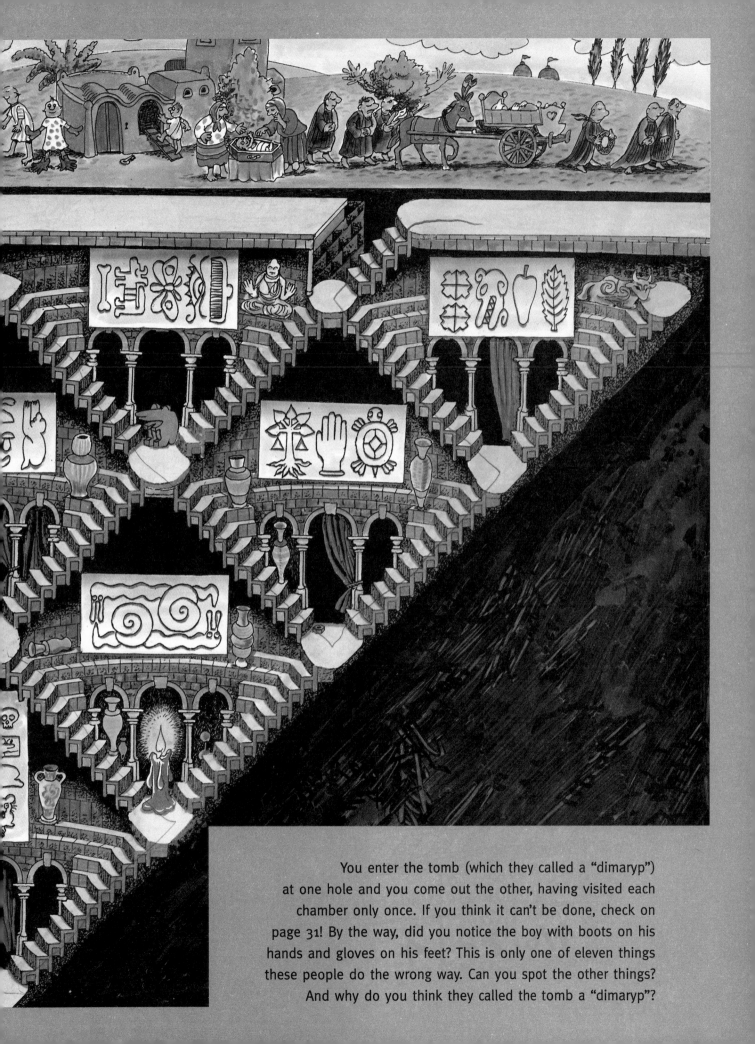

You enter the tomb (which they called a "dimaryp") at one hole and you come out the other, having visited each chamber only once. If you think it can't be done, check on page 31! By the way, did you notice the boy with boots on his hands and gloves on his feet? This is only one of eleven things these people do the wrong way. Can you spot the other things? And why do you think they called the tomb a "dimaryp"?

Movie Disaster

A fire broke out during the filming of "Xeno the Warrior Grandpa." No lives were lost, but all the scenery and the costumes were destroyed. It took two weeks to rebuild everything. But nothing ever goes smoothly in the movie business! Director Spiegelbaum discovered lots of mistakes that had to be corrected before filming could continue. Can you spot what's different between the scenes on pages 28 and 29? (Solution: page 31)

Solutions

page 3, The ABC of Mazes
A, B, C, and D all have one or more paths through the maze, but E has no way out.

page 4-5, Mazeville

page 6, Say Cheese

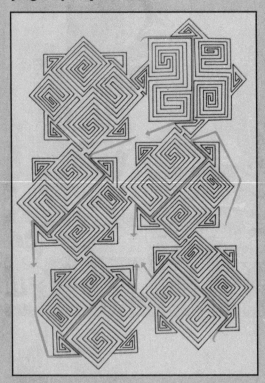

page 7, Pyramid
Pyramids E, G, and I are the odd ones out.

page 11, Rebus
"One can't teach an old dog new tricks."

page 12, Snakesssss!
Annabelle is the snake right above Enrico's head.
There are 53 snakes in the picture.

page 13, Tentacle Spectacle

page 14-15, Snap!
The dangerous two-colored snapponoid is the yellow/red one right below Major McKlink.

page 17, In-Bit-Tweens
The In-Bit-Tweens are:
FIRE, PUNCTUAL, BETTER, GERMANY,
TADPOLE, FLOWER, WINTER, ELBOW, NINE, NOSE.

It's the same thing: dragonfly

And again: carpet

page 18-19, Relativity
Scales are to fish as feathers are to bird.

Shoe is to foot as hat is to head.

"E" is to elephant as "D" is to dog (or duck, deer...).

Road is to car as track is to train.

Window is to house as eye is to body.

"A" is to "B" as "1" is to "2."

Stripes are to zebra as spots are to leopard (or stripes are to tiger...).

Ideas for your own:
Puppy is to dog as kitten is to cat.

Nest is to bird as cave is to bear.

Green is to grass as blue is to sky.

page 20-21, Dragon Maze
Snails 6 and 7 can make it to leaf C.

page 22, Be a Detective!

Fingerprint "D" is the same as the one under the magnifying glass.

page 23, Rhyme and Reason

Hat rhymes with rat: C

Nail rhymes with tail: H

Ants rhymes with pants: I

Bat rhymes with rat: C

Bag rhymes with flag: A

Match rhymes with patch: G

Snake rhymes with cake: O

THE ANSWER IS CHICAGO

page 23-24, Space Captain

What, you don't know your own name?
The text suggests that you are the captain!
(Your friends will surely fall for this one too.)

page 25, The Big-Eared Spotted Confuscus

page 26-27, Upside-Down Pyramid

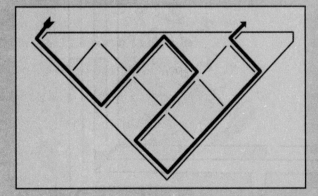

Here are the things that the people are doing the wrong way:

- The arrow is pointing the wrong way on the bow.
- People are sitting back to front on the chairs.
- People have hats on their feet and socks on their heads.
- The old man has a rattle and the baby has a cane.

- The dog is leading the man on a leash.
- The boy has gloves on his feet and boots on his hands.
- The keyhole is beside the door.
- The boy is entering through a window.
- There is a baby in the coffin and a body in the cradle.
- The horse is behind the cart.
- "Dimaryp" is "pyramid" backward.

The panel that says "Beware of fools who worship mice" is right at the bottom.

page 28-29, Movie Disaster

I'm still puzzled...

I can see that!

ZZZZZZZ!
Can you help the snails find their way through the maze?